NAKED IN
PUBLIC

**poems and prayers
from the backlog**

leah juliett

illustrated by ed stockham

Ansel -

Thank you

for everything.

[signature]

NAKED IN
PUBLIC

ISBN 978-0-578-99876-3
First Paperback Edition December 2021

Illustrated by Ed Stockham
Cover Design by Leah Juliett and Ed Stockham
Edited by Karlee Rose North
Dedication Page Illustration by Maggie Mae Rose
Interior Layout by Ansel Nolting
Author Photo by Dana Elaine Photography

Naked in Public is based on the essay written by Leah Juliett which first
appeared in Salty World, January 2021.

Printed in the United States of America

www.leahjuliett.com
www.edstockham.com

:: Listen along to the book ::
Download *Naked in Public* on
Spotify or Apple Music

Baptisms in the Kitchen Sink

Bones in the Bed Frame

+++++++

Buried in the Pit of Alive

++++++++

**"The type of love that I deserve exists
because I exist."**

Taffiny Kablay
@thetribegoddess

To all those who thought they were not meant for living;
to all those who picked up a pen instead of a pipe bomb;
to all those trapped in bludgeoning pit of alive;
to all those who etched their way out of the ache
with holes in their heavy-winged back bones...

to all those caught running with tar-stained heels;
crying in private; naked in public —
to all those whose throats were too strong to hold the holy rope,
and all those who did not think they would make it through the
hot grief of last year —

you did, baby, you did.

Baptisms and Bruised Knees

My mother took me to church during my childhood.

St. Maria Goretti, patron saint of broken bodies,
died at age eleven from being stabbed:
after refusing to have sex with a man twice her age.

Namesake of my childhood church.

I was four the first time I died.
My mother weighs me on grocery store scales
that say I am too big for my age.
My still body is stinted with sexual violence,
sinking me like rock into paper bag.

No matter how much I have bled, I have always felt heavy.
Didn't believe in ghosts until I became one,
until my body became the prayer box
sinners emptied themselves into outside of church.

I think there are parts of me eating up the light inside.

(Grief sits at the bottom of my shoes like pebbles —)
weighing me down like the cross around my mother's neck.

Mom, I'm sorry I was so heavy.
Maria, I think we are two breaks in the same bone —
your father died of malaria,
my father died of depression, though he is still breathing,
I have not seen him alive in years.

(Maybe it is genetic to be walking ghosts)

This is where my legs bent into
spinal cord street lights.

Girls and boys in school walk with twisted limbs.
I wonder if you broke their bodies, too.

When I was fifteen, my partner held me close;
told me they were going to kill themself
thirty minutes before they tried —

that was when I first learned to bury people who were still living.

Now, I find bone fragments in the bibles at church
where I sang apologies instead of hymnals.

Fall on your knees
My knees are rug burned, I'm trying to stand.

Oh hear the angel voices
My mouth is full, I cannot speak.

Oh night divine

Saint Maria, Saint Maria,
I think there are ghosts where my lungs once lived.
I think they are sitting next to my mother in church.

It is July in Italy when Maria is grabbed by her neighbor Alessandro
who tries to rape her.

She screams —
he stabs her eleven times — eleven years old.

When my mother kisses me goodnight,
I wonder if she sees that I am sitting on a crime scene.
I wonder if she looks at me like I may be the culprit.
I wonder if she looks at me.

There are graveyards beneath Maria Goretti,
who fought a fate much like my own.
How do you fight when your hands are too small to make fists?

Saint Maria, Saint Maria.

My spine is a steeple, where I pray to
baptisms and bruised knees,
ages I will never be again,
and ghosts I will never see.

This is where you tore off my skirt.
This is where you crumbled it in the corner.
A stranger would think it was the body of a broken doll,
a broken baby bird
plucked from the bottom of my throat where my voice used to live.

I've been spitting up feathers and hallelujahs ever since.

Before Maria died, she forgave her killer.
I have died many times, and I forgive myself.

SAINT ANTHONY

A prayer:

For when my knees bent beside my sister at the chapel of my mother.
Or, how my gender spelled divorce in the crux of childhood crosses.
Or, the small town where my grandfather wanted to die,
and the smoke-filled apartment where he actually did.

The word of the Lord.

When my mouth is too full of boredom rind,
I will reach past worn lips and remove wet gospel,
wedged under my tongue like the cancer
that ate my grandfather's lung,
and we'll feast together again.

The word of the Lord.

Tell me when the ridges in your leather-skinned hands
are ready to hold me again.
I'm afraid you'll only be ghost-skin by then. All unmarked wood.
I'm afraid you'll only be dog-ended, non-believing,
and you won't believe in me.

The word of the Lord.

Last time I was drunk,
I told my coworker that I wanted to go to her church.
She left a bible on my desk. I left a bible in my mouth.
I'm not sure how to tell her that I don't need God —

I need an excavator.

My bones are built of missing persons and lost things.
I've thought only to destroy myself completely.

This is to say, Mom,
I've been having dreams of falling off my rooftop apartment again.
Eating the ache, exhuming the cavity,
ripping the prayer in which we no longer talk.

I am grateful for the old days —
when the smoke stained your eyes like a burnt egg
and my alcoholism smelled like new asphalt on the long walk home.

I am scorched beyond wound-dressing.
I am scared of the pain that I only know now.

The word of the Lord.
The word of the Lord.

EVEN JEFFREY DAHMER HAS A COUCH

Spring lives in my mother's bedroom —
baby teeth wrapped in plastic cradle her underwear drawer.

With imprint and glue we match mold-to-the-mouth
to reveal same-person.

Before I was taken alive-in-body, my mouth was clean.

I am full of dust-lung and the old cellar door
that leads to bathtub and basement kitchen.

Here, we remove the teeth so the body is unidentifiable.
Here, we pull apart the gums until the mouth-bones fall out.
Here, we tear into fish before throwing her back
into cold river outside Milwaukee.

Your crypt of incisors sit on your nightstand,
where you count-count the girls who were not fully grown:
enamel trophies you scrubbed clean in scalding hot water
and named me the bitter-mouth girl.

You bathed me in acid til' my skin fell off.
All nipple, bare-breast, unbecoming.
You were sewing my scalp to rub on your forefinger,
and wash, wash the bloodstain away.

Now we count-count the newspaper clippings.
With a needle you tattoo your tongue.
I watch as the ink pools the cracks in your teeth,
and you kiss me and turn my gums black.

On the couch in my lover's apartment,
we straddle linoleum trays.
I am watching below as he picks-picks my bones
from his teeth and inside of my head.

Middle-aged men tell me boys from your town,
drip, drip their cellars and wash the girls down.

Drip, drip and wash the girls down.

BRUISED RIBS

I bruised a rib the day you left;
pieced together my body with a hard ache,
and poured salt on my skin as I sang to myself
a drunken chorus of *"you were here once"*.

I miss you like I miss the sky,
and the bed frames that were never mine to keep
and the plans, the plans, the plans.

It's no surprise there was a flood in this town the morning after.

The streets billowed with water as if to say:
you kissed me with a hopeful mouth,
and now you're gone.

The hope dissolved on my tongue and left with a sneaky betrayal.

My ribs ache with loss.

The crack in the bone is full of film:
home-videos of you with her
in the places where you wished me the sky.

These are the empty hands I have now —
the fingers that carefully traced words on your back with the thought
that we had time.

Maybe our hearts weren't meant for this year.
Maybe these beds were only suited to hold our bodies
for a short, short time.

Maybe I misheard your words.
Maybe I misread your eyes.

Maybe I deserve more than crumbs of an uncertain love,
or the scraps of a too-soon stay in the bed of a stranger
at the end of a long, dark night.

I, mad at the door, am without words to say how you could make me
feel so full and so empty so fast.

I withdraw the arguments about spice and time.

There is no one to say who takes the pain
when you & I are gone.

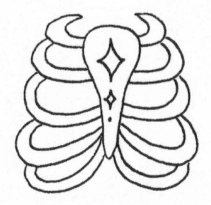

CAVITY

My mother's crow had a cavity in the indent of it's incisor.

For two years she beat it, beat it
against the pulse of hot bedroom on crooked enamel.

Should I have known when you began to clean your teeth
that your mouth was no longer mine?

Should I dismantle my gums with your old toothbrush,
until I am all choking-choking on her tongue
in your mouth?

I am filled with cavities, now;
hoping you return to the familiar smell
of grief and unwashed bone.

Even when mine are falling out, lover,
I will remember your teeth.

CLEAN CHINA

When you first stole my body,
I was too young to watch;
dressed me in white
and played church in my childhood bedroom.

More clean than glass;
I learned that my hands were only good soft.
As coarse as you made me,
it was always my job to be gentle.

A woman is only good gentle.
When the world wreathes in her fingers,
punishes her for temper of men,
it is her job to clean up the glass,

scrub blood from her bluejeans,
show up unbothered,
unscathed by abuse,

tongue taut with silence,
not riddled with rage;
unstained by sorrow —
and fresh like a strange new spring.

When my body was taken
in the hands of a crime,
before my mouth was taught to mold
into neat denial,

before I was strung between loose teeth,
preserved in plastic around my neck;

before my sister and I shared
matching twin beds —

our town seemed so
young, then,
so un-bathed in bone
and nightly news

It's 10:00, do you know where your children are?

They are in their beds,
folded in tight
like fragile eggs
in my grandmother's
baking bowl

(we are careful to keep the air out)

Before the bed felt
so unsafe —

I was clean, too.
I was free, too.

EXCERPTS FROM THE SUICIDE NOTE
I WROTE AT AGE 16
After Doc Luben

1. If you're reading this, it means that something went
   terribly wrong.

2. I am afraid that my eyes are so waterlogged
   that I can no longer see.

3. Sometimes I see my blood in the mouths of strangers;
   sometimes they kiss me and I need new teeth.

   Mom, I can't throw away this mouth or this body;
   the bones that I live in have built me inside a cage
   and I cannot get free.

4. I turn to dust under the feet of strangers.

5. I have a hard time handling things.
   I've been holding matches only to find out
   that I am made of hot glass.

   My brain feels like an open flame.
   My chest feels like red heat.

6. The dark keeps pulling me back to bed.
   Mom, you are afraid I will always miss work.
   I am afraid that there is so much I've missed.

   It is too much for me to catch up.

7. You'll probably think this is dramatic.
   I don't know how else to tell you.

8. I think suicide is misunderstood.

9. It's as if my mouth is open
   and water is being poured down my throat.
   I'm choking and drowning in my own self
   and I cannot escape
   and I cannot breathe.

10. Please don't think you are to blame.
    I've had all the love in the world.

Author's Note: When I was sixteen, I didn't think I'd live to see next year. It's been eight years. I love you. Keep going.

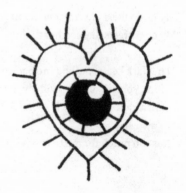

BASEMENT GHOST

There is a ghost
inside the basement
of the head
of my father.

I call him "basement ghost".

When my Dad tells me he is in therapy again,
and no, no it is still not working,
or when he writes sad poems in the notes on his phone,
musing about God and the loss of his children,
I know that basement ghost is climbing up the cellar stairs.

Creaking the concrete, he spills out of my father's mouth —
all white wind and wisp,
fitting snugly in the cracks of his broken lips.

We have met many times before —
me, basement ghost.

The irony is not lost on me that neither my father or I believe in God,
or a morning after,
or a heaven where my grandfather most certainly is not.

He smoked too many Ashfords to not be on fire.

And how, how has it already been four years?

We are all dust and bone in this family,
drawn on old doilies and dining room dishes.

We do not pray for him.

My Dad tells me he was born sick,
that the greatest thing he gave me was a heavy chest,
long before April of 1960.

Dad says our basement is a genealogy map,
says that I will live there too someday.

I am afraid that our houses are too much alike;
floorboards broken in all the same places.

I want to fall through too much, too much some days.

Basement ghost reminds me that I am not alone in this rubber
sadness.
That us two, us two can dance on old concrete.
We will slip in the chips on my mother's old china.
Slicing our skin, we will rebuild this old furnace room
and leave dust prints all over the cavity walls.

"Do not get rid of me"
basement ghost whispers in my ear
every Thursday at the psychotherapist.

"I am the only family history you have"

You are the only history I can carve out of human skin,
and your realtor will never sell a haunted home.

I do not want my father to die,
but I am scared of our shared spirit,
our half-built home.

So I will burn off my hair with Marlboro matches
and set my ghost free through my ears.

This is not a family tradition.

Death is the only thing we have ever had in common —
and so I am boarding the door.

AND WHEN THE CAT IS SPAYED

And when the cat is spayed —
ovaries laid out on cold metal butcher block;
uterus unzipped with ivy-like incision,
and bound back til' bloated belly straddles the counter.

Amen; she is all staple and scar tissue,
shrouded together with scalpel and stitch.

This is the way we weave the animal with the roadway carcass.
The way we arch our backs with the prick, prick of sharp-metal-shame.

This is the way we be empty, we be full,
we be dressed in ice pick and isolation.

We, unfolded; our insides stretched out onto cutting room floor.

And I wish, I wish I, too could be removed of my organs,
stuffed with cotton gauze and grain,
and left to lay still on cold steel.

I am only whole when I am gutted.
Abuse of this body is all that I know to be home.

So I will carve out my small intestine; call this Thanksgiving,
and wrap up this uterus with plastic and prayer;
leftovers for when the bad men come.

When my body returns from the far-away place,
I pray it will be empty.
I pray it will be empty.

HAIKUS FROM QUARANTINING IN MY MOTHER'S HOUSE; CONNECTICUT

March 2020

Ghosted my doctor
to hike up a mountain with
the man who raped me.

Why do I care more
about attention from men
than about healing?

May 2020

ACAB

George Perry Floyd was
killed under knee; nine minutes
twenty-nine seconds.

When 'fuck the police'
sits on my tongue, his name's at
the back of my throat.

July 2020

Met her on Bumble;
we sat in my van and were
too afraid to kiss.

Picked fruit from the yard
and made me a cup of tea
with her mother's leaves.

October 2020

Queer romances end
tragically to remind us
being seen is death.

Dani & Jamie
love each other until she
drowns in lake out back.

December 2020

Had Christmas over
Zoom this year; Dad wrapped gifts &
opened them on screen.

Chewed cheeks; proof of God;
we all survived this year and
will come home again.

July 2021

Ghosted my program
to drink margaritas with
the woman who left.

Why do I care more
about love from a woman
than about healing?

UNDIAGNOSED DEPRESSION ::
A MIDDLE SCHOOL PLAY IN 6 ACTS
After Sabrina Benaim

1. My earliest memory in my childhood bedroom is a rug burned back, that is to say, these scars have been embedded into my skin since before I had words to define them.

We met on TeamJonas.com — that is the fan club where Jonas Brothers fans write erotic fan faction about lives we will never live, and somehow that year, the stories I wrote were all that kept me from the obit section in the front page of my middle school yearbook

2. My mother takes me to therapy in eighth grade. She brings copies of my poems. Tells middle-aged male in leather loafers: "*I don't know why she is so sad. She has so much*". Mom, all I have is sad. Sad is all that does not escape these small-boned fingers; it's been like this since Dad moved. Mom, these poems are not stories I write on the internet, Mom, I swear that this sadness is real. It's a brick in my throat and I cannot choke it down.

3. Girl in my Language Arts class notices my bandaged wrists. I'm not sure whether to shrink or to love the attention. I am a bruised plant on the classroom window; I crumble under human touch while also needing it to survive.

4. Boy I am sure I'm in love with tells me to lose weight to have sex with him behind the high school during track practice. Tells me to shave everything; make myself so little that I am invisible to my own eye. Of course, I do it. The hair clogged up the drain that summer.

I am still cleaning it out ten years later.

5. My parents take me to the neurologist because I keep having tics in my neck, tics in my neck. Mom is sure it's Tourette's.
Doctor tells me: *"this is the body's response to not eating"*.

6. Mom finally finds me a therapist who listens. Does not ask to read my poems, knows this body is a walking crime scene and my metaphors don't need to be scraped from under my fingernails to be analyzed by men who do not know me. She uses big words: Depression. Dysphoria. Dysmorphia. Anorexia. I say these words will not fit in my poems. She says find bigger journals. This is the first time I am not asked to be smaller. I have been living big ever since.

(Middle school did not kill me, but it did not make me stronger. These scars I am still covering with tattoos; still writing notes to the boys who will most certainly never love me back. I am not scared of this body the way I was ten years ago. Rather, I am scared of myself in new ways every day. I am not sure I will survive this summer — but I am growing. I am every day reminded of the girl who got through the thin-ribbed days.

She is me, and I am grateful.
She is me and I am grateful.)

ON CRYING ON THE LAWN OUTSIDE THE
HART SENATE BUILDING; SEPTEMBER 2019

What they don't tell you about working in politics
is that when the personal is done being political,
it is only personal.

When the ghosts quit hiding in your bed frame —
they are just ghosts,
no longer family.

You will stand on the ledge of your sixth floor office
and only think of the cool impact of the marble
beneath your shattered face.

In another story, you will not jump.
You will not, will not
ruin your mother's Christmas dinner.

In another story, you will go home
to your clockwork bed and
only know God —

you will go home to your eggshell apartment and
only know God.

It is possible that the worst version
of this story is the one where
you both do not jump and do not go home —
you are stuck in your skin and he is not there
and he is not there
and he is not there.

A PRAYER :: FOR GABBY PETITO & THE MISSING AND MURDERED GIRLS IN THIS TOWN

Hallelujah, amen.
For every girl that claws her way out
of a white transit van
in Moab.

Hallelujah, amen.
For every defensive fist
assimilated as angst and aggression;
for every bruised arm and sliced cheek
caressed on a police pad
to never see the light of day.

Hallelujah, amen.
For the too-anxious-to-sleep-alone;
she sleeps with a man whose hands
only feel warm wrapped
around her neck,
her words wrapped
around her tongue
when she is asked by her mother
who causes the bruises, again

Hallelujah, amen.
For the hurt, the hurt
passed off as quiet squabbles
and dumb teenage dread.

Hallelujah, amen.

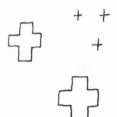

For the watch bearer; for the breaker of silence;
for the girl who says too much, too much
and leaves only to be dragged back
by the nails again.

Hallelujah, amen.
When the girl becomes gravedigger;
when she watches the hole in which she will be buried
from six feet away at the foot of her friend.

Hallelujah, amen.
When she knows that her body
will bear it's last breath
in a forest in western Wyoming;

when she knows that her body
will bear it's last breath
at the hands of the man
she'd defend.

Hallelujah, amen.
For the girls whose mother's kitchen cupboards
read only prayer cards, now,
may your holy hands wash only clean dishes;
may your fingers be splintered-no-more,
may the boys, may the boys let go of your wrists,
may your shackles be empty,
may the mass in your memory be
full of still-alive, still-alive.

May you be, still-alive, still-alive.
Hallelujah, amen. Hallelujah, amen.

GHOST IN THE WALL DAY CAMP

To the ones I loved who did not stay ——
you are the ghosts in the walls of my childhood bedroom.

With every hot match on my thigh;
burnt my skin to repent for your leaving.

Wore my mother's wedding dress in a haunted dream of you
until I wake up all shattering.

It's morning again in America.

I don't know how to dry flowers in the spines of old books
so I hang them on bed frames
and remember the nights we held each other
in the middle of a storm ——
you are the lightening and I am the frightened child,
always told that the dark attracts heat.
Now I'm burdened under heavy thoughts of me
feeling your warm skin,
your light like an eggshell under a battered whisk you break.

You say you aren't capable of loving me the way I need to be.
I am taken aback by the sharp pepper on your tongue.

I have never imagined a room where you weren't there to fill it,
so now you live in my walls.

With the cracking foundation you come back in shadows,
old visions of you filling your side of the bed,
reclaiming the handprints you left
on the wine glass by the nighttable.

I am fully incapable of forgetting,
so my drunken tongue calls you when you should be out with her.

I tell you that I cannot leave you and you ask me who is calling.

How quickly we forget the bones we left behind.
How quickly we forget a promise.
How quickly my walls fill with old film
until I cannot see you anymore.

I am terrified I am to leave this old bedroom
where you are no longer here
and I can no longer see you.

But I know I need to move on.

So I will.

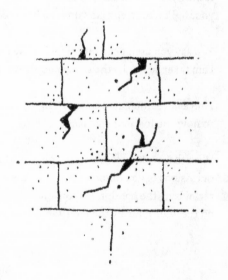

QUORA HEADLINES IN MY INBOX
WHICH ARE ALSO POEMS

"My Mom Gave Birth to Me at 40.
Is it Possible that I was a Mistake? I am 15."

"Is it a crime to shoot someone who is sneaking into your house?
I am 15."

"Did Mary Really Tell Freddie Mercury She Was Pregnant?
And do I have to tell my mother?
I am 15."

"Why shouldn't I have my teeth removed and replaced with artificial teeth
that I don't have to brush?"

"What do you do when you know you're becoming evil?"

"What is it like to get kicked out of Harvard?"
"What is it like to get kicked out of Heaven?"

"What is it like to get kicked out?"
"What is it like to get kicked out for being outed?"

What is it like to only feel the kick?
Not the gut, or the roof of the mouth around swollen tongue?

I think the killer in the town next door
is the same boy who scrubs my inbox.

I think he reads my emails.
I think he's in my emails —
that is to say, I think he sees me.

Quora Headlines in My Inbox Which Are Also Poems:

"Is it possible for a baby to be born before the water breaks?"

"Have you ever applauded an act of vigilante justice?"

And aren't these two the same?
To be born into a world without water;
to be born fist-first and still be thirsty for air.

Some days I am afraid that I will drive into traffic
when I am reminded of the town
that still holds my home.

That is to say, some days I am afraid of losing my home,
and this blistering skin;
afraid of the next ten years of morning after's
and sad walks home from the house of the girl who can not,
can not love me.

Quora Headlines in My Inbox Which Are Also Poems:

"Have you ever exposed yourself in public? If so, why did you do it?"
"Have you ever been exposed in public? If so, who did it?"
"Have you ever been naked in public?"

Breathes deeply. Makes fist full of pepper and air.

How can I say that I was exposed every time I kissed you?
How can I say that I remain exposed, even now that you're gone?

PHOEBE BRIDGERS CALLS THIS MOTION SICKNESS
BUT I THINK I JUST WANT TO DIE SOMETIMES

When bisexual cowboy Phoebe Bridgers says:
"I hate you for what you did, and I miss you like a little kid" —

I am reminded of how
your abuse of power
left me stunted at an age
that I no longer belong to.

You, older than my mother when she birthed me,
know too well that I am not equipped
for the growing pains you caused.

I, haunted at the door
of every ghost-lover
whose bed I have shared
(even the ones that I fucked on the phone).

I, distracted by the body you left behind
and the rooms we filled together,
stood staring out the kitchen window
long after you'd left.

I, blowing glass into boxes
where I put disappointment
at how you once again, once again
led me to believe that this would be different.

The men in this town are as bad as their wives;
cut holes in my chest and then leave with the knives,
cut holes and then leave with the knives.

LATE JULY WOUND DRESSING

It's the pavement in August that traps us.

It's the thinking of old people while sleeping with new people;
how it burns at the back of our throats
because we know that we shouldn't.

You slipped out her name like a key;
unzipped my bones and once again we are in that hotel room.

It's the head-to-the-heater in late July.
It's the cracking of knuckles under the bruising of ribs;
how we penetrate the wound with the constant undressing.

I am so bare-foot under thoughts of you with her
that I cannot hold my shattered chest —
only glass slips out of my sternum;
our brilliant nights are now unexceptional in your head and memory, still

It's the wine corks I kept in my bag;
trinkets from another Monday night last summer.
It's the tight-believing that there would be
another night, another month;
how the months now pass with no call.

I am going to get through this year,
but not without thoughts of you
constantly on the other end of my tongue.

I am wired for silence to help me forget.
I am silent to help me forget.

AWAKENING :: SEVEN YEARS LATER

And in an alternate universe where we both still exist / you still love me / in the nuanced way your guilty mouth allows / I fumble rusty fingers to hold you tighter than I should / the ghosts in your gut don't press your achey joints the way they did in the old bed / we cling to cold walls / hot bodies too wet with grief to clutch in sweet-dark pretend / as if to say, we pretend this love will make it through July / we pretend not to see the blood under our chewed nails / that the bite marks are sexy ways to hold the taste on our tongues / when we're both already long gone / assuming ourselves too heavy to hold / too young to see trauma as more than wounds to hide and hold and swallow / ghosts to rack our heads until we both are convinced / we were never meant for this year.

And in an alternate universe where we both still exist / we don't suffocate / don't pretend we can love one another to life / don't spit serotonin deep down our throats / deep down our smokey lungs / we are not thick-chain burdened / not an empty wrist / not a shell of liability that cannot exist in the light of day / as if to say, I can love you without saving you / I can hold you without making you sick / care without clinging / I do not want you in a world where you do not want yourself / I do not want a world where you do not want yourself / there are stars that have been dead much longer than us / that are still hot enough to be seen / you told me yourself / there are ghosts that have been apart much longer than us / that are still loved enough to be seen.

THANKSGIVING

Death threw me a baby shower this summer. It kneeled at the crook of my neck in the shape of the homemade belt loop my father no longer wears. I exhaled and my throat exited the cold wooden bed frame. A woman-voice ripped from my larynx, and I haven't seen it since.

Mental illness is the cold turkey my family always forgets to serve — broiled in broth of hushed tongue, sitting angry in the oven. Mother snaps steel gate closed before the smell gets out. I am rotting depression in young adult wrapping. I am gender and grey matter and hardly here.

I am here — hardly.　　

My mother's mother's fish-eyed breast was taken off last Sunday. We call this holy, mastectomy, as if we call this mass. As if all the mouths I've kissed are healthy.

This empty pelvis is the garbage we forgot to take out for three weeks last fall. Maggots spilled out on cracked blacktop — crawling up the legs of my sister. These are the burdens that continue to eat her. The smell of bone dust has stayed on my body much longer. I am crooked cervix and misgendered medical records. I am too heavy for a chest this thin.

My childhood bedroom has become both gravedigger and priest — mourning me and calling me holy; pouring dirt over childless ovaries and burying them outside my bedroom window so I can never forget what my body can't grow. When my mother prayed for skinny girl, she got girl who does not believe in prayer, prayer who does not believe in girl. That is to say, she got me.

My pelvis has begun to sprung telephone wire. Doctor calls them cysts and opens my legs to the smell of old food that rots in the garbage disposal that we feed to the living and ask why they're dead.

Now there is a churchyard in my small intestine where poisoned people to continue to live. The rotting, the asthma, the babies dancing on my clavicle — etching their names onto my taste buds and filling me with their garden breath. Mother says this is the price I pay for not being woman. This is the price I pay for not being man.

My God, why can't I be both?

A thousand years of shamed sisters pound against this uterus; try to breathe it back to life like a man-made oxygen. This is the birthday party I never had. All these ghosts, all these souls I've known. All these holes in my elbows too sharp for wide men to fit in. They make game of their entry and call it holy ceremony.

My father held me over boiling water when he moved close to Boston. I can never quite tell when my back starts to burn. But I am trying to build more sensitive skin. More holy words. Maybe birds find shelter in new wombs where they are not slut-shamed or devoured for their meat, and perhaps this body is much more real than these feathers disguise me to be.

These splinted talons made to pray to the child I'll never carry...

Now I flee, force-fisted, barefoot into the mouths of the men whose names sit stagnant at the foot of the nation. A hand full of dirt and a throat full of larva, teaching my insides to grow.

This year the dysphoria did not sit cold in the oven. It marinated the whole house. It was the maggots, the turkey, the dirty broth and all my family.

It hung the hand-me-down cross at the top of the bed frame. Stretched around my neck like my grandmother's pearls, like my grandfather's unmarked grave.

Now every bite of this jaw is reliving my mother's church.

But my voice is too large for this infant casket, this half-built home.
When grief strangled me, my throat strangled back, screaming:

I am banshee body. I am watery grave.
I am uncomfortable, I am unearthly, but I am here.

Until the morgue turns over and the bones spill out.
I, half-shadow, half-child, half-nothing-of-a-gender,
dancing among decaying bodies
like a strange and summer snowstorm.

My voice will not die; I will not die:

Today I break the wishbone like a stillborn amen, painted in prayer
and grief and goodness. Today I burn the birth certificate — eat the
echo, celebrate the parts of me the world will never see. Singing
"where have all the children gone!"

Spitting my hell in the face of the structure; screaming:

I am the holiday my body has always loved to live in.

THE ARTIST

To the Boy Who Posted My Naked Pictures Online:

Thank you —
for showing me that trauma need not live on your bones,
but can hide on the web and still burn the same.

For turning my organs into strands of telephone wire;
eyes: catalogues of coffins to live in;
mouth: damaged hard drive.

I began to think of suicide
like the light switch in my chronic depression —
close enough to reach if I could just get out of bed.

We were texting once.
You told me I looked like a starry night.

"Your body was painted by Vincent Van Gogh,
please show me a glimpse of your private art show"

I said no.

You begged for over a year.

Exhausted under light of my phone screen,
and under the weight of your raunchy request,
I undressed.

Picked up my paintbrush and with shaky hands told you:
"I've never shown something so pure".
So you said with allure,

"I'm sure it will be a masterpiece".

I sent you still-frame screenshots of my shallow stomach,
the pale lumps of fat called my breasts;
my face sitting fearful in every photograph.

I told you to lock them in your personal gallery;
plant them like seeds in your bone-dry garden
so as they could not grow higher than I could see them.

But somehow the seeds sprouted all over town:
teenage boys would bend down,
cut my flowers with sharp scissors and keep them in their jean
pockets.

Now everyone has seen me.

That morning I grew glass menagerie limbs
and smashed them on every sharp surface
so as to make myself disintegrate,
but my fragile fourteen-year-old flesh
will forever flourish on Firefox or Google Chrome —
sprouting like weeds from mynonconsentedclitoris.com.

My pixelated pink parts forever stretched into sensual screensavers
for over-sexed teenage boys
who sold my body like a trading card you
can't. buy. back.

The girls in this town call it *revenge porn* —
as if to live in this body could warrant revenge.

I was fifteen...
and I trusted my art in the hands of a thief.

But Van Gogh gave his paintings away for free
just so someone would see him —
now you've seen too much.

Though nonconsensual visibility still leaves me unseen —
I'm left grieving a body taken from me .

But...
When the boy who posted my naked pictures online
locked me in a cyber shame,
he forgot to lock my voice.
My real bare art.
I swear to God, I have never been as naked as I am right now.

When Picasso's paintings were stolen from a Florida gallery,
they were recovered.

I will recover.

My breasts hang lower now; I walk much slower now.
My waist is bigger now; I speak with vigor now.
I have no gender now; naked surrender now,

I am free.

I take back my tongue and I learn how to speak.
Take my art back with gallantry, stop being meek.
My body, electric, is free from the thief.

Now the girl in the pictures is forever to see...

But the joke's on the thief,
because she isn't me.

Now the girl in the pictures is forever to see...

But the joke's on the thief,
because she isn't me.

ON EATING THE WHISTLE
FROM THE BAD MAN NEXT DOOR

And when the headache gets too loud—

Death march of a drum between two ears
and endless waves of grain— America.

There is no grief if it is not the grief that strokes the lines of my belly;
if it does not pierce the curve of my tongue,
it is not meant to smolder my skin.

When we count the blessings we can live with,
we count the people who burned us twice,
meaning, we count the grief and the scar;
the leather and bone.

I am not meant for a chest this wide.
I am not meant for a feeling this big.

I am only gut-open on cold deli-block,
where men graze my body for meat
and itch the discomfort out of my skin.
This is the way of Long Island.
This is the head of the stone.
This is the rye in my belly;
the twisted pleasure of making love to Her for the very first time
and feeling like a full red moon.

This is the half of myself I gave back;
these are the cracks in my palm where I carved out the bad-men
and the bibles where I swore off their violence.

These are the dry hands;
these are the oils she gives me.

We are rosemary and orange peel and new soap.
We are more than we are in the dark.

I am only chest-full at the lonely side of road;
before the cars whisk me like a new egg;
before the fixing of brakes and stroking of hair
with a match-in-finger under bare foot pedal-stuck, America.

Men stick to me like trauma sticks to the bottom of my feet;
I drag them around and leave dirty footprints
on my mother's linoleum floor.
She changes the tile, but my feet can't get clean.
With detergent and grace, we strip grease from my toes
and call it trauma therapy.

I am a walking blood-buzz.
I am a young group of thieves.
I am the new bed with the new woman who fills my belly
and the bad night with the bad man who purged me.
I am old, tired memories and new drunk friends.
I am here and I am glowing.

I was born tongue-tied-taught to a country
that showed me that showing up is more important than looking in;
more ripe to make it home alive than to make it out of home.

I know too well the men waiting to exile my bones
at the other side of these sharpened keys do not want to kill me
like the man who already did.

He made a nest in my head and returned to my door
with birds in his mouth and blood in his teeth.
I am not afraid of their feathers or their whistle
or their incessant fluttering.
They live in my throat.
I open my mouth and their drunk chirpings
spill, spill out.

I am not built of nighttime sidewalk, but I tender-fear myself,
America.

We eat in my room like a church-time prayer;
with freckled laughter we piece back together the lives
that were stripped on dust and dumb-broke bed frame.

We are not afraid of what has happened to us.

I have never had the words to tell my mother
that I am afraid of heights the way I am still afraid of men—
not for what they could do to me
but out of fear of what I'd do to myself alone with them.
How I'd let them eat me.
How I have.
How I continue to.
How I only exhale debris and guilt and shattering
bare-foot-fingers of them as they run away in the dark, friend.

Even in this softness I scream for the taught ripple of alive
to hold tight to my lungs when I can finally exhale
into a good, safe bed, with a bright-sun woman
who calls me baby and doesn't ask me to mark my blessings on
on the bedpost.

She does not wish me small.
She does not make these deli-feelings louder.
I save myself from the butcher block and return to her sheets.
I make good of the highway.
I sing light into Her and into the whiskey pot.
I mark my words twice.

She does not wish me small.
She does not make these deli-feelings louder.
I save myself from the butcher block and return to her sheets.
I make good of the highway.

I sing light into Her and into the whiskey pot.
I mark my words twice.

She does not wish me small.
She does not make these deli-feelings louder.
I save myself from the butcher block and return to her sheets.
I make good of the highway.
I sing light into Her and into the whiskey pot.
I mark my words twice.

I have not driven through doubt.
I have not eaten away at these feelings,
yet I am scared to make light of them.
I am scared to take them underwater with me.
I am scared of the shelter they provide,
hiding in the cool shadow
where my belly doesn't see the sky.

This week I tattoo my hands when I see Him
dragging his bike on the other side of the road;
He is walking with neighborhood kids.
They make light of my window tint.
I stick to my shoe-leather-seats, scared of Him,
even in knowing I can crush him with my car
and with my tender thighs.
I still hide from the boys in my town like a high school crush;
we exchange phone numbers and I never call.
I am too afraid of admitting my feelings in public.
I trade zip codes and wish the whistle out of my throat.

Hallelujah, amen, America.

And when the headache gets too loud —
I stumble out of the brick bed;
I talk with my hands;

I accept gentle kisses and return them like a new, sweet fruit.
I take Her home with me and do not count my footsteps.
There is no dirt on the kitchen floor.
The silence isn't heavy, and my body isn't bone.
We do not dance through grief.
We take long, hot baths in sad subjects.

My thighs are wet like small pools on a new life beach, America.

Yet the whistle in my throat still rings.
The bird sounds still spill out.
I swallow the guilt and eat the shame heavy-down.
I will only accept a hum.
I will only accept a faint whisper of hurt, as if to say:
this trauma will live with me, but it will not control my voice.
This fever isn't forever.
These men won't take my keys.
This dark won't steal my very good light.

I am a quilt of non-believing;
I am a castle made of stone.
I am not the hard things.
I am not the deli-block.
This grief is not mine.
This burn is not scalding.
My feet are all-clean.
The dust is all-gone;
my lungs are clear, not heavy.
 I am not a beggar for grace.
I am not an angry consequence.
My guilt is not a silo.
My trauma is not an echo that I cannot sift through like a new sky.

I forgive myself;
I sing with the birds instead of shaming them
and I do not think of Him.

I cry. I cry into the clean floor.
I exhume the old crimes in front of my new self.
I spend the day in bed with Her.
I usher in breakfast.
I feel pleasure and safety and it's sexy.
I am not a punishment for a burden that was never mine to carry.

And so, and so, and so.

I will not bury myself in the bedsheets;
I will drink spicy margaritas
and let the pepper sit in my center-throat.

I will love so queer I will build myself back.
I will love and build myself back.

OPEN LETTER TO SHAME

Shame, the way we feel it;
the way we exist in it.

The way it wholly envelops our skin
until we struggle to see beyond it's high stone walls.

Shame, ate me alive when I was fourteen.
Shame, full and aching, shame.
Bones popped out of party dress — shame.
I did not eat because my mother's bird bones
were smaller than mine — shame.

This is not the mouth I wanted to close.
This is the way I did not want to be seen.

But I am here, wide with abandon,
shouting mouthfuls of sorries to the girl
I hid inside the bedroom closet for too long.

No, don't come out if you love women,
No, don't come out if you don't fully think you are one.

Shame — ate my insides with a childhood hunger.
Shame — the party ghost I always let stay in my bed sheets.
Shame — who told me I did not deserve to be on this stage.

Told me: *you are an apology, and no one wants to listen.*
Told me: *it is no measure to have lived and lost,*
you are better off not alive at all.

Shame, I made it —
I am alive in spite of you.

I am wide and big and loud and here:
in all of my ruthless glory,
I made it.

Even when you turned the lights out on the bedside table.
Even when you begged the bad men to my childhood door.

Shame, I forgive you —
but I am done waiting for you to allow me to say:

I am here.

THE WOMEN VOTED THIS YEAR

This year —

We fought the bad men who pulled our skirts and called us quiet
while slowly sticking sharp fingers on our tongues,
pressing voices hard under huge-headed-hand;
we squirmed under silence,
we billowed.

We, whose stories riddle protest signs and prayer marches;
we, whose advent is not only now coming
but has been here for generations.

We ate the bad men; ate the grief;
ate those that claimed that our bodies were failing,
that our worth was once priced on the work of small men,
that the women who worked wouldn't hold higher office,
that the girl who'd been raped had asked for it, again.

She: who knew nothing of pain til her gender betrayed her.
He: knowing nothing of us but our will to be small.

We, who are not easy made into silence.
We, using our voices and being un-still.
We, with our hands out and chests cracked from climbing,
are taking The Office and Capitol Hill.

Now is our garden,
our time ever-blooming,
to reclaim our spaces
and swallow their hands.

They, who have choked us
with bleak perseverance;
on their old grounding is where we shall stand.

We, the believers,
who've never forgotten,
that life, liberty,
of a red, white, and blue;

We, who unbounded and resurrected,
stood up to the bad men and shouted #MeToo.

This year we aren't quiet,
amending our textbooks,
unwriting our ghost lines and strict gender roles.

No matter our gender, our race or our difference,
this year we will gathered and marched to the polls.

The women voted this year ...

did you?

THE TINDER GIRL IS SICK ::
A PLAY IN 6 ACTS

I.

When I told you I loved you after our second date,
I did not, did not think that this was my depression
climbing out of my mouth and into my phone screen;
my bitten nails weak from heavy-handed drink
on heavy-handed barstool in my country-western hometown pub,
in which I sang karaoke without feeling my throat;
you climbed into my throat, I mean into my bed,
I mean into my mother's spare bedroom bed.

This is not an excuse for loving you so deeply so soon,
this is only excuse for trying.

II.

When I told you I loved you after only knowing you for six days,
I did not, did not believe I could be this clouded,
this clouded by mental illness.

But there is no good way to tell you that the Tinder girl is sick,
that she will attach to you like dust mite under fitted bed sheet;
just two young-college-nothings sharing bitter lip joke,
bitter bourbon — maybe I can't remember what you drank,
maybe that's the price of it all —
happened too fast, too soon,
it was a swipe in the dark that we even met.

Why am I conditioned to think that this, too must mean something?

We are in your car, and you pull from your e-cigarette
before putting your hands on my neck,
and I don't pull away.

I, only akin to loving a strong drag of nicotine and violence;
opening ovens, not scared by the smell of heat and gasoline,
not turned off by your stale breath kiss.

And with heavenly abandon you leave moths in my mouth,
moths in my mouth;
I've been unraveling my clothes with my teeth ever since.

I am not scared to say that this two-day-love almost killed me.

III.

When I told you I loved you over the phone
while pissing in my bathroom sink,
you respond: *"you do not know me"*,
"this is not healthy".

And maybe,
maybe that's a half-cocked way of saying it back.
Because girl after girl have always wanted me sick,
told me I was better chest-broken,
knees bent;
easier to fill with twisted fingers,
wood-worn lips —
easier to choke out the root of the spine.

But this is not an unrequited love poem.

This is not an obit for how you did not comment
on my stretch marked stomach.
No, there was nothing bent-backed about my rough skin
under your cold touch;
now you live in Vermont
and I am nothing.

IV.

When I deleted your number
and then proceeded to drunk message you on Instagram
until you responded: *"please stop texting me"*,
I did not see this as invasive.
I did not think I needed help,
that love is not supposed to be this way.
I did not, did not think I was chasing a falling
glass plate
from the high-up shelf.

V.

When I am still thinking of you longer than I ever knew you,
I fail to remember that my diagnosis makes me this way.
This is not an excuse, this is a prescription;
a receipt that reads maybe,
maybe I was looking for something in you
that had nothing to do with you.

And now, now my stomach is still empty.
My chest is still hollow, spine semi-supine on the floor
of my mother's first house.
The smell of cigarettes and breakfast still stain my pillow.

You have been gone for two years.
I've missed you longer than we ever talked.
And maybe this is what we inherit from sick parents,
or maybe I am just too much, too much.
So, I will stop writing you.
I will misplace my phone in the cold wash of morning after,
not text you when I'm drunk, knowing full well you are still the only
person I want to talk to.
I am still the only person you do not want to talk to.
And that is okay.
I will live with that.
I will learn to live with that.

VI.

It has been two years since I spoke your name
in my whole-belly one room apartment.
I, no longer caught on the rubber couch of forgiving someone
who did not, did not want me.
My pillow no longer smells of menthol,
my breath of smoke,
hot from fire in my small intestine.

I am healing the parts of me you wanted dead,
clearing out the grave and removing all the small-parts.
My wasted liver no longer drinks.

I no longer wish you were near.
I no longer wish you were near.

ASEXUAL EROTIC LOVE POEM

Dear Lexapro,
Or, An asexual erotic love poem;
Or, explaining to my lover why I can't be touched back;
Or, the ways in which staying alive
means putting to death my most intimate parts.

I.
I was born feet first, cesarean-style like my sister;
my first ache was breaking of water, breeching of cervix;
I was home-made hemorrhage before my mother knew my first
name.
I, medicine cabinet built of white wood and gold-bottle garland,
stretching around my neck like a newspaper headline, as if to say:
depression is my greatest inheritance;
my missing front tooth.

We are all medicine-mouth in this family.

II.
I am eighteen and my doctor deals me dosage of a terminal
treatment, tells me: *"this will take the feeling out of feeling"*.
Let me tell you: nothing takes the guilt
out of wishing you could answer with a moan
from a trigger finger on a loaded labia.

III.
The side effects for Lexapro include:
fainting, seizures, nausea, and lower libido.
Doctor tells me: *"better to be sick than to be sick"*
and *"darling you are dry but you're not dying"*.

IV.

I haven't had pleasurable sex in five years,
that is to say that I am twenty-four years old
and the last time I remember feeling something in my vagina
was when it wasn't my choice.
This is not to say that my bed hasn't been warm,
rather, I am colder with a hot finger wedged inside me
than most are my age.

V.

Amen to the medicine cabinet that is both a prayer
and preacher's pharmacy.
Amen to keeping myself alive in my own palm-pressed hand; understand
that when I swallow it is not a surrender,
it is a full belly and a dry mouth.
In this body the choice between sexuality and vitality
is a thin line of gold bottles and torn skin.

VI.

I am not ashamed that I can't have sex,
don't want to have sex,
can't feel sex;
that the most erotic part of my evening is staying alive;
loosening the belt loop
and forgetting the ache of a hard hit.

VII.

Maybe my body isn't meant to open damned and dripping,
but bare and still-boned;
I swear that statues are most powerful
when they too are made of stone.

Maybe I am also meant to be admired and never touched.

Dear Lexapro,
Maybe this dryness is also a prayer.
Maybe I am also a prayer

FREEDOM CELL

I find the lump beneath left nipple and I do not grieve.
I ask my shallow cysts,
this tissue be too tough,
too tough not to slice.

I ache to exile this chest;
unbenign these un-cancer cells.

We do not worship the day where the slate was made clean.

MORNING AGAIN IN AMERICA

It's morning again in America
when young white male
drives ten straight hours
from South Allen, Texas
to an El Paso Walmart,
where he shoots and kills twenty-two people.

President of the United States says:
"mental illness and hatred pulled the trigger, not the gun".

And isn't this also a poem?

In which my mental illness is so bathed in bleach
that it almost is not trigger warning?

In which my "President" is so bathed in bleach
that you almost, in his hand, miss the gun?

ELECTION SEASON

And when my gender ate itself out of my stomach,
climbed up from my right lung
and mouthed the word *"trans"*,
I was not afraid.

Instead, I stuck out my tongue like children on snow days,
peeling back skin from my always-chapped lips,
and waited for the left shoe to drop .

It took five years.

I spent summer with breast-binding on bedroom carpet,
with pieces of fishbone and father and fear,
of the politicization of my holy body
at the hands of a man who
cannot spell my name.

I tell my mother I am not afraid —
watch as my stomach builds itself full
of ballots and bruises,
campaign contributions;
left lung collapses from steady pollution.

This is not a pristine referendum.
This is government-mandated order to breathe...
ovaries fitting in loose childhood teeth.

This is both sides of being sewn shut.

I, whose body demands to be woman;
I, who demand to be both.

Writing my breasts a discharge petition;
signature not with the name I was born in;
wringing my wrists with wet constitution.

This is heaven before unholy took office;
this is hell from a person on fire.

I am caught in the smoke in-between —
thighs clenched between God and a hard GOP.
Institutionalized, both have control of my body,
and my salmon bones,
that November.
We mourned a democracy we never had,
that November.

Grieved gender and bullets;
grieved trans body bullets;
grieved trans body bag ballots,
Green Party bullets —
amen, referendum amen.

We are grown now.
We make harness of wetness,
make pen out of paint chip,
and make ourselves out of this thin constitution
that tells us our liberty ain't justice for all —
just for some.

So, we swallow,
a crowning oppression ,
colonial construct —

of private and public,
of he, she, and they.
Is piss on these kneecaps my absentee ballot?
My bathroom, my cloture, my rights signed away?

My veto?
My coup?
My common law body?
My mother, mastectomy, lesbian, gay?

I am stronger
than government cardstock,
than a plastic betrayal of lives I can't live.

I am more
Than this state-made surveillance;
non-binary body;
the personification of hate others give.

These traumas, these triumphs, these micro-aggressions,
these binary lenses and strict gender-roles.
The blood and the ballots and pain circumvallate;
these bodies boxed up and then sent to the polls.

We, people, we, soldiers,
We, plain resurrection,
We, left in the baptism water to chill.
These voices, these tongues,
these, the beds we grew up in
will never be silenced
or exiled,
or killed.

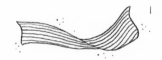

We will never be made to feel small... no.
We will never be voted away.

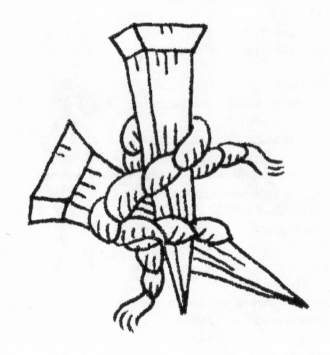

SHE, TOO, AMERICA

After Langston Hughes

And when my mother's daughter departed cracked ribs,
did she know the legacy that her womb would weave?

Cold child, bent-necked, alive, and hollow-hearted,
aching with abuse, riddled with a sticky pain .

When men on wooden boats deemed her heavy and uncertain,
she flew her valiant flags and processed the freedom marches.
Dawned with the anthem of an awesome abolition;
alive, with the glory, republic.

Whose body held the banner across Selma's Edmund Pettus;
who watches Ellis Island with a torch all drenched in wine;
who when planes pierced New York Harbor, invited them to dinner,
and she sang *Amazing Grace* to those gone before their time.

Whose spirit crushed, the November we elected hate to office,
when fire bruised California and our nation set ablaze.
When protest took the streets of a war-torn Minnesota,
we took a knee and with abandon, read off all their names.

Glory,
freedom,
iron-jawed angel.

She whose rape made headlines or whose body never found.
Indigenous, Latinx, or Black woman lost in labor,
She —trans or non-conforming — who the world won't hear a sound.

She, Anita Hill.
Christine Blasey Ford .
She, Breonna Taylor.
She, Vanessa Guillen.

She, too, America, faithful and forgotten,
and when the world recovers,
will be holy once more.

AMAZING GRACE (HOW SWEET THE SOUND)

The world is cracking in my ribcage, and I cannot breathe.
But the fire inside tells me to speak, so I will.

My grandmother's religion cannot explain the sick society
in which man holds man against woman,
holds woman against gun,
holds gun against head
and pulls the trigger.

We are the trigger.

In a country where the right to vote is harder to obtain
than the right to bear arms —
how many women did we lose to violence tonight?

The Violence Against Women Act was signed into law in 1994.
 It expired last year, and the Senate will not reauthorize it
because of the powerful gun lobby
which believes firearms are more precious
than the lives of my sisters.

But we rise up.

For Atatiana Jefferson.
For Ana Grace Marquez-Green.
For Korryn Gaines.
For Taya Ashton.

Amazing grace how sweet the sound;
was blind but now I see.

SIX FEET

And when the world is well again,
we will pull back our bootstraps,
empty our lungs.
Spring clean the cupboards,
cough up weeds and stream water
stuck in our superior lobes.

We will frequent fruit baskets; strawberries ripe
to where loneliness lies too-often in the bed next door.

We will rise from our sheets, we will grip tighter doorknobs,
we will grip tighter neighbors who share in our grief that
young doctor up-street did not make it out of bed last night.

We will grip tighter bakers and grocery store workers
who leave flour cups brimming cold white on our outside porches
for those times when the bucket runs low;
for those times when we are too afraid to venture out
into coldness of town.

We, who were once too full to hold copper pennies;
too quiet to whistle.
Our own breath too much, too much of a threat to our lover's safety.

With touch too hot, too hot we hold children with towels and prayer.
Sewing fear into medicine masks that fly high
over the towns we grew up in —
schools we grew up in now closed for the summer and fall.
When we as a nation, who, sick with oppression,
are now sick with a lightness that rattles our gall.

For those, who could raise a hand in spite of a heavy chest;
in spite of a swelling tongue,
of a slowing breath.

And when the world is well again,
we will touch tips of fingers whose skin was once clear and callow,
lining our lips with sugar from the full shelves.

We will cough only clean air.
We will not miss our neighbors;
they are sitting at our kitchen sink
cutting strawberries,
arranging peace lilies,
begging the children to once more,
once more wash their little hands.

We suckle cough syrup out of habit;
laughing and dusting off aprons at the sounds of 8:00 bells.
The city is at it again,
dancing flashlights and drums
to reminders that once we were alone.

We will pull at our desk lamps,
the flick they will give.

And with prayer and six feet, we will live.

BURIED

in the

PIT OF

ALIVE

WOMAN IN THE COMMENT SECTION
ON FACEBOOK

Woman in the comment section on Facebook tells me
America is no place for "queers".

That I, born with locked jaw and a glass chest,
am unworthy of wearing any sash but one made of shame.

Dear Women Who Think That I Do Not Deserve To Be Here:

I birthed my identity the way my mother birthed me:
hips twisted, head breached.
I have learned to make home of this shallow body,
That is to say, I have learned to walk on broken bones
and hot pavement,
knee-deep under notion
that when I, fat and queer, with nothing of a gender
wake up to the women in the comment section on Facebook,
I am not unbothered.
Rather, I have learned that progress is painful,
that existing in boxes where you are not welcome
does not mean finding another box, rather, punching bigger holes; using
louder words.

I will use louder words, so you cannot unhear me
when I tell you that I deserve to be here.

On every page on Facebook.

And every comment section will shake with my name.
I am here, with hellfire and bent knees.
And God damn it, I'm not leaving.

NEW AMERICAN FUNERAL
(IF YOU REALLY WANT TO KILL ME, MAKE IT GOOD)

A funeral, in which the eulogies are internet comments
that I've received since going public with my sexual trauma:

1. *I think she made it up.*
   Who could violate that thing?
   The guy who did it was probably drunk.

2. *I would click away if I saw her naked, LOL.*

3. *Why are all lesbians I know fat or ugly or both?*
   I can't believe she has even had sex — who would do that?

4. *She has a dog face — woof.*

5. *Male, female, or mentally ill?*
   Ugly looking chicks disgust me —sorry for having standards.

6. *Dyed hair bulldyke — must be a feminist.*

7. *She's an idiot; nobody wants to see your fat ass anyway.*
   Take the blame on yourself and stop using a fucking scapegoat.

8. *You're a disgusting person;*
   you deserve to die.

When I die,
by my hand or hand of God,
I will hang upside down on the cross in my grandmother's garden,
buried among the herbs and hydroponics;

my eyelids stretched back become porcelain pots
for maggots and magnolias —
lard and lipids slip off my skin-suit
and I, too am made of bone.

The word of the Lord.

Contrary to what incels on the Internet may think,
they do not make me want to die.

Instead, they make me hungry.

Make me eat their words with rotten teeth and sharp tongue;
swallow down a wooden throat and let them gravel in my gut —
but glass can't digest like bones can.

And there is nothing more sharp than a ghost word
on a flat-feathered body.

I am full-bellied and bent-necked,
I am mad and I am growing.
Cutting up my insides, unzipping my organs,
let them drip, drip down me, wet and wide-legged
like a slow-growing cancer.

This is the New American Funeral.
This is the atrophy of internet anonymity;
the pulse of a hot, florid flame on a body made of dirt and dead skin.

I am all nipple and bone.
I am censored and sanitized for careful consumption.
I am poison and pulp on a dead leather highway.

I am two blurry eyes and a voice made of stone.

I am dog face, I am dog face,
that is to say I am open mouth and sharp teeth.

I am disgusting,
I am dripping from my wrists,
cracked-knuckle finger sandwich,
and bone, and bone.

I am bearded vaginal rupture.
I am aching, I am aching,
cracked chest but I am breathing,
I am breathing.

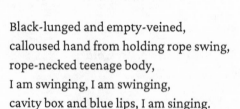

Black-lunged and empty-veined,
calloused hand from holding rope swing,
rope-necked teenage body,
I am swinging, I am swinging,
cavity box and blue lips, I am singing.

I am swallowed by a rugged gum bitten to the pulpit;
I am held down underwater til' my holy-skin swells.

The word of the Lord.

The problem with men who try to kill me on the Internet
is that they don't come prepared to hunt the beast that is this body;
the hellfire that is my ravaged tongue.

Dick too dull to pierce this blistering skin-suit,
this molding mouth.

This curdled collar too thick for small men to choke me.

I am tooth without rot,
knife without handle;
etching my insides until I am all scar — no tissue.

My God, my God, I am starving,
my God I love the taste of small men.

My God, I love beasts that fit in the curve of my gums
so I can pluck, pluck their fucking fibulas with my fat fingers.

If you *really* want to kill me make it good.
Make it a blade-to-throat terror;
twisted arm and broken bone.

Make it binge-worthy so the audience enjoys it.

And then eulogize my shame.
And then cut me where the vein shows.
And then empty out the contents of my body on the mantle.

Dare my bulldyke ass to peel back your spine with my teeth —
watch me sew my wrists back together with your coccyx;
baby, I will drown you using only my thighs,
crowning your cortex til' your comments on my body
stream out of your left eardrum —
til' your stomach churns salt water and slut shaming.

Baby, don't mistake my hunger for anger,
or my lockjaw for silence,
or my silence for holy commitment.

Mama, take me to my grandmother's garden.
Let me bury myself among weeds and the wood wasps.
Maybe this will be the end of a hard year,
or a too-long silence,
or a silo in which my patriotism will never be questioned
because there is nothing more American
than being slut-shamed on the Internet
by a half-mannered boy who takes hold of this body
and claims it as home.

A funeral, in which I am still alive and can write my own eulogies:

1. I was a blessed child of God,
   even a God that I could no longer see
   and didn't know how to believe in.

2. I was not what strangers wrote about me on the Internet.
   I was fat, I was slutty, but I was real.

3. I was not afraid to die.
   I was not afraid to die.

NOTES FROM A NIGHT SKY IN CONNECTICUT

First of all — fuck you
for dimming my light
by opening your sky full of stars in my hands
and then turning my world inside-out.

I have only known dark black for so long, so long,
that when you turned on the lamp,
I thought it was a new moon;
silly not to realize that you held the cord
in your hands.

You, eager to pull the plug from behind the bed frame
and run into the arms
of another fragile moth
in love with your heat;
fully unaware that she, too
will be trapped in the bulb.

We are both bright with believing
in a God who cannot see us.

We were both bright with believing in you.

First of all — fuck you
for allowing me to unravel my ripe bones
into your shallow bucket;
not knowing you'd brought a hatchet
to a garden party.

I opened up my bed to you
and you shredded the sheets —
but not before you made my body adjust
to your cold-blooded hands on my neck.

This is not to say I am angry that you left me,
rather, I am angry that I could position myself so vulnerable
to another petty thief,
disguised as a woman worthy of my grief
in her splintered-finger hands.

I, cold at the party,
bare in a fever of your missed calls
and my missed messages.

I am too young to believe in someone
so jaded by hope and democracy.

Baby, when I am elected,
I will block your number.

You are the type to come back around
and cling to the burn of my
great success —

and I am the type
not to let you.

PUNKS DON'T DIE AT THE HANDS
OF AMERICAN ASSHOLES

Tattooing my cats' names
on these hard-ass knuckles
was the most punk thing I did
that year —

the rest of the time
I spent sheltered beneath twin beds,
my ginger-heart broken
by a bold American asshole.

Tonight I drove up East —
sat in the front row of a hell-woman show.

(She breathed bone and blonde hair.)

We dance to depression rock
and I forget you exist.

Watching bugs die in the sharp heat
of stadium strobes
reminds me a little of you...

I dare you get close to my glow again. I dare you to come near.
Pulverize your skin until you are
no-longer person —
only skeleton with a fist in your mouth.

I call every man in my phone when I'm drunk;
vomit in the hands of my friends.

I tell them that I'm leaving the poison parts of me behind
for them to clean up with the garden hose
in the hot light of day.

(This may be a confession of alcoholism
but I'll never admit my addictions in public).

On every first date I am asked if I'll write
a poem for a stranger who'll leave me that night.

There is no better poem
than I write to my bones
every day by waking alive.

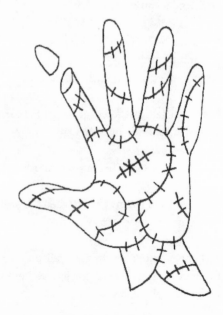

TO THE MEN WHO TRY TO FLIRT WITH ME (AFTER I SAY I'M GAY)

To the men who try to flirt with me (after I say I'm gay):
Why?

Does this way of saying "*no*" carry too much weight to understand?

Or, is my sexuality a challenge,
a token to rub between your fingers,
as if to say my legs will only open
upon being rubbed up between your fingers ?

Or; your pride is fragile like a plate in my hands;
I eat from it, take from it and you expect
something in return.
As if to say, I cannot be fed without first saying thank you.
Opening up my body to you is the only way to say thank you.
You deserve me and I cannot object.

When we held hands at the bar,
(me and my girl not me and you because
honey I would never hold your hand),
when we held hands at the bar
and you asked to take us both home that night,
did you see our outward display of affection
as a meal for your consumption?

You, plucking the thought of me from your teeth
like you'd already swallowed me whole.

Why is it my burden to learn how to say no
in a way that you will understand?

I tattoo *"dyke"* on my neck.
That still doesn't keep you away, you say:
"You are the prettiest dyke I've met"

You say:

"I'll take you to bed, fuck you how your girlfriend couldn't"
"Fuck you how a woman wouldn't" you say
words laced so tightly with violence
that my middle fingers turn purple.

Men, whose confidence so capacious for someone whose
comprehension runs so shallow in my hands.

I am fodder under your feet.
I am a walking supper table;
you take from me, take from me
until my wooden legs give in,
until I'm more cracked than holy,
more drunk with my discomfort
than you are drunk with wine.

When I say I'm gay,
this is not an invitation for you to convince me otherwise.
This is not an invitation to my home address.
The bed is not made for you.
My cup is not empty for you to fill it.
I know deeply who I am even when she's not here...

I know deeply who I am,
so maybe you shouldn't be either.

CARRY THAT WEIGHT

When Columbia University student
Emma Sulcowitcz
began carrying the mattress
on which she was raped
on her college campus
in 2014,

she ignited a movement that
bore the burden
of sexual violence for
silenced students
worldwide.

The weight of
fifty pounds of foam
trembles
against the cost carried
by victims of
campus rape.

When laid atop by	When laid atop by
His hard body,	His hard body,
imprint of personhood	imprint of personhood
remains embedded	remains embedded
in the structure of	in
the memory foam.	me.

Why must the weight of sexual trauma always be mine to carry?
Why must the weight of His hands on my neck never be mine
to forget?

SCREEN ACTORS GUILD

I call these tits
the Screen Actors Guild
because man after man
in my internet comments
reminds me of
how much I
sag.

Me, heavier than your sock
the morning after spending night alone,
am all milk-duct and mammary gland —
a gluttony for gravity;
ribbed tight with orchid stretch marks
and areola bumps.

The year that
Catherine O'Hara
took home the SAG Award
for outstanding female comedy —
I felt cheated;
baffled by how any woman
could make men laugh
at her expense
more than
me.

(I will cut off my nipples
and suffocate men
who time after time
say I'm heavy again;
in time I'll be heavy again)

THE POET TAKES A SELFIE

Bends wrist;
positions phone on the ledge of the rear-facing window
to get the best bedroom light.

It is 5:15 in this city; golden hour.
Makeup meticulous.
Pink nails to match my hair,
pink hair to match my eyeshadow, to match the
daunting tire but sleepless eye sockets
can't hide that I was manic again last night.

Stayed up all night to rewrite in my head
all of the things that I wanted to say
but didn't —
all of the things
you told me, be honest
I couldn't —
too scared to tell you in the moment,
but now the moment's gone.

Sets timer *3-2-1*

Click.
I am in my sister's bedroom.
The light hits my cheekbone
and you cannot see
how heavy-soul I feel.

My god, she is all red dress
off the shoulder to show sex appeal.

The sadness doesn't matter if the selfie
doesn't show it.

Click.
Dyed my hair red;
thought, maybe if I transform myself
into someone I don't recognize, the pain
in my chest won't recognize me either.

Click.
Sent this selfie to a rebound.
Butterfly filter decorates my nose,
hides how hollow I feel
to talk to somebody new.

Click.
Did not shower for two weeks;
hope messy hair is sexy.

Click.
Stayed on the bathroom floor
for too long after
this photo was taken.

Click.
I am back in my bedroom,
the morning after you tell me
to bring you your clothes;
tell me you need your hoodie
but don't need me anymore.

I have never felt more trampled.

Click.
It's been days since we talked and something feels different;
I'm starting to worry your feelings have changed.

Click.
Took this in my car on my way to work.
That night we got sushi and shared a scorpion bowl
and a hotel room;
that sex was good sex
and we both know it.

Click.
Took this the day we got pizza
and they gave us raw dough
and shisheto peppers you couldn't eat.
Do you remember how I laughed at you
for telling the waiter they were too spicy?

Click.
It is two days before we met.
I can see in my own naive eyes lack of hurt,
like I don't even know what's coming.

Click.
Selfie from the day I pierced my lower lip.
It will fall out eating fajitas on our first date.

Click.
This is a day sometime before we met,
and I am certain that if there was a before,
there will also be an after.

Click.
When you said it wasn't fair to me
to not know how you feel.
When you said not knowing how you feel
also tells you how you feel.
And I said: *"It's okay"*.
What I really meant to say was that
I don't know how I could feel so strongly so fast
and you feel nothing at all.

Click.
I am in in line at a funeral,
waiting to see the bloated body,
surrounded by collages of photos,
moments of still-alive and priceless time before.
I tell my sister:

"If I die first
Please post pictures of me
Where I look truly happy."

She says: *"I don't think you've taken them yet."*

Click.
You tell me that you understood why your ex left you
when you had to decide to leave me.
I don't know what to do with that.

Click.
The poet takes a selfie
And it is only a selfie.
It doesn't mean anything.
And (I know now) neither did we.

QUESTIONS FOR PEOPLE
WHO DON'T LIKE MY POEMS

1. Does my honesty make you uncomfortable? When I spread my legs wide / open myself to the grief and invite you in, too / when truth weighs heavy / like a dog at the end of a tight leash on my lips / when I spit in the face of the men who tell me that my words do not matter / do you wish I had swallowed my tongue / swallowed the truth caught tight to my throat / rather it ruminate in these bones / and this belly?

2. Do you not believe me / when I tell you the ways in which this fragile world has hurt me?/ Think your skin too smooth to make / so sharp a cut? / You, trusting the glass from which / you drink wine until it slices your lip / I, trusting the men I let into my bed until / they slice these hands in the name of holding / no, my body is not grateful to be a graveyard / for men that claimed to be holy.

3. Is my nuanced attempt to / clean my bones of this heavy / too obvious to be true? / Am I too obvious to be true?

4. Are these words just / toenail clippings / in the bin of doesn't matter? / Are you just going to flush them, too / after I am gone?

ODE TO THE MEN WHO CALL ME FAT ON TIK TOK

Ode to the Men who Call me Fat on Tik Tok:

Yes — and?

I don't think you know that I also have a mirror;
that I can see that the curves in my body
run deeper than the insincere lines that you feed your girl.

Baby, maybe this body is thicker than Brooklyn smog .
Maybe this chest is full of my weighted-down heart;
I'm not hurt by men who point out the obvious,
as if fat is a slur
and I am a pure-cherub child.

Not sure what your goal is here,
as if to call me big will make me silent.

Honey no money could
pay off my voice.

So let me remind you:

This body is a celebration.
This body is a holiday in June.
This body can't fit in small hands — maybe get bigger arms
to hold the weight of the joy that I carry.

When you call me fat,
I wonder if you have been born with new eyes,
That you must walk around and declare the obvious.

So let me help you out:

Call me hell-fire.
Call me undaunted in my courageous pursuit of hard things.
Call me bigger than Midas;
louder than a bomb in the hands of a child .

But sure, call me fat,
as if your words will make me weak.

Baby I'm strong,
not in spite of your words, but because of them.

Not in spite of this body,
but because of it.

WHEN MY RAPIST LIKES ME ON TINDER
After Kevin Kantor

When my rapist likes me on Tinder,
my body feels like the State of California —
we are both burning alive.

I am in bed, under-sheet safety is all that I know,
clutching phone in my hand,
my screen is a glow stick in a pool on a hot day this summer;
it happened this summer.
Now September is here and the film in my head
is still stuck on this scene,
it is all that I know.

He is there,
in the background of every picture.
Haunting every bedroom...
all the girls in this town have his name in their phones —
to the right is an eggplant emoji.

It started on Snapchat.
That is to say, I don't even have his number.
That is to say, he never gave me his number.
Now my phone is filled with unfiltered messages,
pictures of him in bed where I am now,
clutching my phone like a bomb.

When my rapist likes me on Tinder,
I am reminded of the hard pain between my thighs.
I am reminded of vocalizing the pain,
against every instinct or rule I was taught.

Good girls are always taught silence;
make ourselves small while pretending to be bigger
so the hole doesn't hurt.
 I say *"it hurts"*
he says *"that's because I'm doing it right;*
you've never had it right".

When my rapist likes me on Tinder,
I am just a body.

I think I left my skin in that bed.
I am under his fingernails,
he under mine.

My sister tells me to wash the comforter.
My boss tells me to take time off.
I am stuck in that room.
Now he's stuck in my phone.

I swipe right —
afraid of what could happen if I once more deny him.
He does not message me.
I don't know if I expect him to.
I don't know what I am expected to do.

When my rapist likes me on Tinder,
I delete the app; start using Bumble.
I cremate my phone. I
 cremate this body.
I am dust in the cup of whiskey I drank
at the end of the bad, bad night.

am afraid this body is more crime than human now.
I am afraid that I am more crime than human now.

To the Rapist who Liked me on Tinder,

I have taken so long to write this
because I know you would say it's not true.

It *is* true.

And I'll never forget —
and I'll never let you forget.

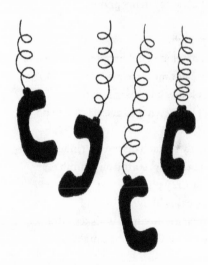

BODY COUNT

A normal conversation on Facebook Messenger in 2010, 13 years old:

1. *Are you a whore?* He asks with such conviction,
   on my chest is sewn a target
   before I have time to think.

2. *My friend told me you'd give him a hand job. Is that true?*
   I consider you a friend, I swear I do, and you're pretty.

3. *Whatever you were wearing looked good and*
   it made your tits look nice lmfao not being perverted.

4. *What's the most you have done with a guy?*

5. *I could take you out somewhere. You should really see my dick.*
   What size bra do you wear? You could be naked for a while;
   promise this is our secret.
   I think u will never forget what we are gonna do.

6. *You're a dirty girl and I like it.*

7. *I'm gonna lay you hard.*
   I'm gonna suck your face so good that you will need a break.

8. *I wish I had someone to comfort me and my dick;*
   you should be that someone.
   You could rub my boner.

9. Hey sexy, hey, hey, what's up, hey, hey reply when you get this, do you still have a cell, hey Leah, you looked pretty good today, hey, hey, hey, why do you hate me, what's good cutie, what's your body count, you still a little whore, you still a little whore, I miss you, when can we chill?

10. *People say you're a major slut and I want you to know I like you.*

I was groomed to believe that my body was useless if it wasn't a cavern for ravenous men / young skin, my only capital, the only thing I owned / the only thing of substance in my rotted infant bones / She, a vessel for virile control in the shell of a childish naive / a uniform beggar for teenage regard / testosterone candy / licked the head of a penis before she was full-grown / before I was full grown / let them jack off to the jpeg of me vulnerable as a bird's nest in the palm of a bear / he was a bear / now he's just a blip on the phone of a profile I've blocked but I can't get him out of my head / Is this what it feels like to be born captive? / mutilated by misconduct / mangled in the sour stomach of sex crime / we were both too young to know what was happening / I was too young to know what was happening / this is to say, I was the slut at the bottom of the Halloween bag / the body count, the body count / the names and numbers of boys I banged etched into my fragile forehead / my sullied skull full of guilt and grievance / Mom took my phone away for a year, grounded me from going outside, couldn't look me in the eyes the whole month of December / never told me, never told me, darling your body is nobody's ashtray / nobody's termite home / this slander, this damage has damn near drained the youth from your eyes / the flame from your throat / don't be silent, don't be silent / baby, let's call you schoolboy, let's call you daughter, let's call you anything but slut, anything but slut /

Hey, hey sexy, hey, hey, you looked pretty good today. Do you want to suck my dick? What's your body count? What's your bra size? Want to rub my boner? Want to stoke my ego? Want to let me fill you with my false-hope dick?

I promise you will never forget what we are going to do.
I promise you will never forget what we are going to do.

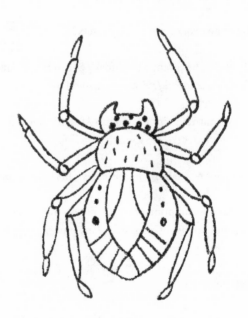

NOTES ON NAMING MY ABUSER

Tomorrow marks four years
since #MeToo went viral —
and I still have not named my abuser.

In every interview / I am first asked / when I will name him / why I
have not named him / what does his name look like on my tongue /
how can I prove what happened / if I refuse to name him / what does
it mean for breakers of silence / if I refuse to break mine?

Why is the world / so consumed / with vilifying him /
that they forget / to sanctify me?

Why is the world / so confused / with my silence?
I have already shared / so much.

Is nobody concerned for my safety?

They'd rather point a pitchfork / at a nameless man /
than break bread / with a woman on fire.

They'd rather point a handgun / at a nameless man /
than give thanks / to a woman on fire.

I will not name him / in this elegy / his name is not mine to carry.

If your consumption of me / relies on the destruction of him /
you will not be satisfied with / my mouth.

I will not use it to destroy another man / like another man has
destroyed me.

NOBODY'S VICTIM
After Carrie Goldberg

And after Googling my name for the fourth time this morning
(which I know I should not do)
it has become apparent that the Internet
thinks me synonymous with victim.

In every article,
author meticulously mentions
how I walked into the mouth of a bear
without first discussing
how bear was birthed
in the bedroom of
his mother;
with every lesson on
collecting honey
from the fragile hands of bees
he learned that
his desire for sweetness
was worth more
than my safety.

I, sticky in the claws of a beast,
did not get stuck in my mother's womb
to be reduced to
somebody's victim.

When I walked out of the mouth of the bear, alive,
I proved that I am stronger than sharp teeth
and a gnarling gut.

When I swallowed the savage
that swallowed me,
(with words and not with violence)
I proved that
I am more than the rape,
more than the worst things that ever happened to me,
more than the bad day that has become the only day,
more than the trauma porn that news websites
make me out to be;

Surviving sexual violence is not
the most noteworthy thing that I have ever done.

Calling me
somebody's victim
makes it easy to forget
that I belong to nobody but myself.

When we romanticize Bundy
and Dahmer
and the men who
killed me in high school
(and this summer);
when we paint them a soft smile
not a sharp set of teeth ...

How easy it is to forget
that someone like me
had a life before they
ended it.

How easy it is for someone like me — to have a life to be ended.

LIFE CYCLE OF A MOTH

I am a clean child —
obsessed with holding onto things
until long after the novelty has worn off.

Twilight books: read them
Grocery lists: kept them
Letters from my dad in his birthday cards: pressed them

Until the paper is moldy-yellow I will
cradle them in my grease-filled hands;
the ink is no longer legible but I know
that this meant something somewhere.

We meant something somewhere;

in one piece of time you were every new meal
that I would keep sitting out on the counter 'til the meat got cold;
always contemplating whether digging in ravenous
would make the roof of my mouth too akin to the taste —

knowing something is just around the corner
always satisfies my hunger more than opening it up
in the light and letting it die too soon.

This is to say, I always need my birthday gifts
to stay wrapped, long, long after I know what they are —
it is safer to keep something from leaving too early
if it is trapped in a wooden box,
if it is folded in the memory of "it hasn't happened yet".

Some adult moths live their whole lives in the span of a week —

in the grand scheme of things, I think we were
no more fragile than an old moth in the hot
light of a ceiling fan.

This is to say, maybe I should have kept us safe in the chrysalides —
never opened up to you,
never let myself touch you with eager, unclean hands —
maybe that would've kept us alive much longer.

I am akin to holding dead things in my fingers —
all these grocery list obituaries clutter my car,
but I keep them stuck to my skin because they meant something
in one alternate reality.

You meant something in one alternate reality.

And maybe in that same, strange place
you still exist,

dancing in clean sheets
like a greedy sadness snowstorm.

I will keep you there,
dried in the spine of an old book
because I cannot let that alive-feeling go,
no matter how much I tell myself
it's long past time.

My defense memory tells me it's long past time —

A moth will die in an instant
just by brushing itself against an open flame —

I'm still not sure if I was the fire or the burnt wing,
all I know is that the pain of losing something
before you're ready to let it go
is always hot and aching and too-soon.

In the end, I suppose pinning a dead thing in place
is the most humane way to preserve it;

I get to keep an empty-shell body
until long after I am ready to let it go,
and you get to continue to exist
somewhere entirely new.

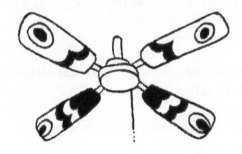

NAKED IN PUBLIC

Man at the bar likes my tattoos.
Takes his finger,
traces it along the gravestone on my left bicep,
not knowing he, too, will soon be buried underground .

Man takes out his phone.
Leans over my barstool and opens his camera,
situates the lens between my black bra straps —
my chest on his screen and I am exposed.

Tells me: *"don't worry, I'm gay".*
I say: *"this is not the first time I have been made to feel bare
by a confident man in a nightclub".*

He asks if the words on my throat have a meaning.
I say: *"they'd mean fuck you if I could redraw the ink".*

My body — I say in my head of course,
because I don't have the nerve on my lips —
my body is not a prayer for you to recite.

Just because I decorate my skin does not make me consumable.
Just because I taste good,
look good,
just because I am haunted, doesn't mean
 I am a ghost;
cannot be walked through,
looked through,
touched without my consent.

Please don't capture me in pictures so I cannot see myself.
Please don't minimize my body so I cannot see myself.

I've been trapped in the photos of men for too long,
It is like I've been naked in public.

I take a sip of my drink.
My shame is the heaviest thing on this barstool.

I let him take the picture.

I am still alive on the phone of a stranger in Connecticut —

and I will be long after I'm gone.

UNFINISHED

When Tik Tok user who will not be named
comments on my suicide poem
telling me I should have *"finished the job"*.

I am reminded why I am so bless-ed alive.

Why my arms, strung together with ghosts and live-wire
refuse to sink back into old razor tub.

And these thighs, thick with burnt cigarette scar,
continue to run,
shifting on shoe leather and hot chub-rub,
fistful into the next day.

When I was fifteen, a man took me to bed
while my parents vacationed down South.
When the moon snuck out of my bedroom-view window
just long enough to make me feel lonely,
I woke up, drew a bath,
watched myself bleed in hot water.

Begrudgingly boy got out of bed,
called me attention whore,
and left with the warm air.

I was first-time reminded that night
that wanting to kill yourself is too deep a burden
for boys who only want to love a warm body.
But I don't know how else to call out for help
when my voice is still trapped in the tub.

When I tell you that the thought of an early exit
has always been more comforting
than the other side of a cold pillow —
do not paint me dramatic;
do not paint me starved for views.

When I tell you that I left my first job out of college —
my first real, adult job out of college —
because I couldn't look out on the sixth-floor veranda
without dreaming of jumping onto cold marble first...

I know that life is worth living
because I have seen the blood in the bathtub,
I have felt the cold tile of the bottom floor.
I know that pain is only as agonizing as the next day
when it does not come.
I know that moment between waking up and remembering
is so, so fleeting,
but that moment becomes a collection of moments,
and those moments become days,
and those days become years,
and one day you're alive and it's eight years later,
and that boy lives in a new state,
maybe the one your parents vacationed to
that hot summer
and one day in September you decide to write a poem
sharing your suicide note that by God,
you never had to send
and a stranger thinks he can tell you
that you should have finished the job.

Baby, I am. With every breath. I refuse to leave this job unfinished.
I refuse to leave this world ... unfinished.

SAINT SLUT

And on the fourth day / when God created the Slut / He did so in His mother's image / wrapped Her in white, thigh-high exposed, small lips, suggestive smirk / a tempting poison wrapped in fresh alive / dripping wet in spite of a dry mouth.

And when He created the Slut / caressed Her in His heavenly hands / this is the last time that He'd touch her clean / She is always dirty now.

In His grief / pressed a knife in Her palm / a wreath of burning lilies / the first sign of Her boiling body is the smell of smoke and violence.

The year that Monica Lewinsky was gutted in public was the year that I was born /

We both knew too young the feeling of being carved alive / canonized at the feet of men / gagged / made an example / put to death by our own salacious image / no expectation of resurrection / left to die in public and expected to forgive our killer / that's what saints do / that's what women do / born to absolve the sins of men until they choke us with them / until they spread our legs with scandals and take their turns trying us on / rewriting our gospels in their name / tabloids to tell how they slept in the bed of a martyr / we weren't as good as the rumors said we'd be / a waste of heavenly body / a waste of human life / we're too akin to garbage / too moth-eaten to marry / no good holy / they made us secular beasts / born bleeding in the name of God / only knowing sharp pain now.

I gave up on God the year the men in my town painted me hungry and decided themselves fitted to fill me / called me genesis /

✝

disrobed my teenage body and dressed me in the image of God /
scalped and tortured without my knowledge or consent / a ring of
thieves to pass me like a Sunday host / let me sit on their tongues and
dissolve / it's holy to worship a Saint / even in the basement of a
burning church /

Hallelujah / I am no longer withheld suffering / by this body / I deny
the men who were bless-ed tempted to eat me alive / and brand their
names in my throat / rape me, shame me, leave me a jilted prayer / I
reject the testament which claims I was only born to be feasted on / I
refuse to romanticize forgiveness / I refuse to romanticize the people
who killed me / I will not absolve their abuse at the hands of
potential to return / I will not allow loneliness to keep me begging at
the door of someday / as if to say, someday the people who handed
me grief and expected me gracious will make their righteous return
to once again bulldoze my body and leave me with pins in my mouth

I am not an acquittal to fill the holes of lonely boys / I am not an
example / I am not a graveyard for broken men / I am not gone / I am
not gone /

Hallelujah / I am breaking the chain / removing the knife / burying
the lilies in the garden out back / the scars in these hands are holier
than all of the men in this town / more cracked than the chapel where
we first met / where you told me I made you believe in God again /

And on the fourth day / when God created the Slut / He made sure
She would stay tethered / both by shame and memory / rage and
terror / She cannot leave what lives inside of Her / who She really is
when She's alone with God / when She's alone with herself / She
cannot forgive what does not belong to Her / She cannot let go of
what only belongs to Her / She cannot leave with a burdened chest /
amen /

Amen / I forgive that which does not belong to me / I set down this
weight / I release who has bound me / you were never mine to carry / I
am the God I needed / built only of goodness / honoring only myself /
burning no-one / hurting no-one / bludgeoning the burden /
resurrecting the rage / grieving, plenty / shouting, holy ::

I miss you / but I will not return to you /
I have more than this / I am more than this.

PLACES I'VE FOUND GOD
After Michelle Awad

In the driveway of my childhood home / in the women who praise each other's bodies in the bathroom of the bar who are too drunk to mean anything that isn't true / at the hot end of a cigarette / in a language barrier / in the head of a mouse / in borrowed socks / at alcoholics anonymous / in forgiving assholes / in blind grace / in worship music that sounds like punk music / in a plane ride over a city at night / in clapping when you land / in needless forgiveness / at mass with my grandmother on Christmas Eve / in a warm bedroom under a weighted blanket / in the blood in my underwear / in a chapel on wheels / at Mohegan Sun / in your mother / in my father / in quitting my job and listing the reasons why / at a tattoo shop / in the number seven / in messy faith / in fearless love / in cats with human names / in daisies dyed blue / in community organizing and grassroots political movements / on Election night / in freckles and acne scars / on the shower floor / when driving in the snow on Idlewood Road / in love on the kitchen floor / in rage screaming / in primal devastation / in listening / in sobriety / in radical softness / in tarot cards / in butterflies and birds and rivers and roads / in asking for help / on New Year's Eve / on Christmas Day / at my therapist's office / in clean sheets / in a glowing chest / in the moments when colonized time does not matter / in my stretch-marked stomach / in the solar plexus / in waking up before you do / in staying awake until the black fades out of the sky / at the Boston Marathon / in the breakfast after a funeral / at an intervention / in arguments with my mother / in the hand-written messages on my grandfather's paintings that hang in the living room of my father's house / in essential workers/ in justice / in K-12 teachers / in grocery store checkout lines / on family Zoom calls / in feeling seen / in tears / in self-love / in community love / in reckless, sloppy, scary love / in healing / in growing / in tripping over religion / in accidental saints / in a person that is also a mirror / in talking to my sister / in hospice for dogs / in looking at someone and saying "oh, there you are" / in everyday miracles / in unbridled courage / in you, in me, in us

ACKNOWLEDGEMENTS and *THANKS*

I'd like to extend my unending gratitude to my dad for always showing up for me, talking about hard things, sharing his joy, love of words, sorrow, and support through all the years and through all the bad things.

I am grateful to my mother for always challenging me, pushing me, and holding me accountable; for always asking that I show up as my best self and loving me through my worst selves. Endless gratitude to my kitten-children Piper, River Jane, and Tarly Binx for keeping me alive when I wanted to leave the world.
I love you so much I could burst.

Thank you to all of my family members for your deep love and support, and unending thanks to my sister for being my lifelong friend and always allowing me to play all the sad Jonas Brothers songs on the car radio. You rock.

To our team at March Against Revenge Porn — I am forever indebted to you for the reminder that I am not alone. I am lucky to organize and fight injustice with a team of such badass survivors. We are doing the thing.

To my Connecticut Youth Slam Poetry family and the 2016 Connetic Word Youth Slam Team: thank you for making space for me, for hearing me, for reading the gritty first drafts of my work (including some of the pieces in this book) and for introducing me to spoken word.

Thank you to all those who have financially or emotionally supported my work and who have always been there to listen when I thought I was too much, too much — I am not.

Thank you to Joelle and Tom and Gabi who saved my life during my freshman year of college in a small dorm room in Connecticut. Without you, I wouldn't have made it to this year. I love you and I'm grateful to you. No matter where you are in the world, I will never forget what you did for me that year.

I love you. Let's keep going.

ABOUT THE AUTHOR

Leah Juliett is an internationally award-winning writer, speaker, organizer, and activist. Leah is the Founder of March Against Revenge Porn, a global advocacy nonprofit and justice campaign fighting tech-based sexual abuse and digital domestic violence. For their work, Leah has been featured worldwide in print and media platforms like CNN, NBC, MTV, BBC, CTV, Sky News, BuzzFeed, TIMESUP, *Huff Post*, Billboard, and *Teen Vogue*. Their work has been published in multiple languages and received global regard and recognition. Leah's writing has been featured in national and international publications like *Glamour Magazine*, *Seventeen Magazine*, *Happiful Magazine,* MTV News, GLAAD, and various literary journals and magazines. Leah has been recognized as a L'Oreal Paris Woman of Worth, *Glamour Magazine* College Woman of the Year, George H.W. Bush Daily Point of Light, *The Advocate* Champion of Pride, Delta Airlines Accelerating Acceptance grant winner, and GLAAD Rising Star. Leah is a two-time TED speaker and has spoken at universities and conferences around the world, most notably at The Human Rights Campaign Time to Thrive Conference, The Kennedy Center for the Performing Arts, Thomson Reuters, University of Minnesota School of Law, New York City Hall, and The GLAAD Media Awards.

Leah fundamentally believes in civil rights, social and environmental justice, messy religion, recycled shame, faith without fear, and unabashed love. They live in Connecticut with their cat-children Piper James and River Jane. For more, please visit **www.leahjuliett.com** or **www.marchagainstrevengeporn.org**

CPSIA information can be obtained
at www.ICGtesting.com
Printed in the USA
FSHW012312281221
87250FS